Illustrated History of
MARTIAL ARTS

KARATE

by Kevin K. Casey

illustrated by Jean Dixon

THE ROURKE CORPORATION, INC.
VERO BEACH, FL 32964

ACKNOWLEDGMENTS

I am grateful to Sensei Lee Gray and Okinawa Karate & Kobudo of America. I also thank Sensei Ray Meier and the Bushido-Kan Martial Arts Academy.

PHOTO CREDITS

Diane Covalt: pages 15, 20, 22, 23, 26

Library of Congress Cataloging-in-Publication Data

Casey, Kevin, 1967-
      Karate / by Kevin Casey.
          p.   cm. — (Illustrated history of martial arts)
      Includes index.
      ISBN 0-86593-366-9
          1. Karate—Juvenile literature. [1. Karate.] I. Title. II. Series.
   GV1114.3.C37   1994
   796.8'153—dc20   94-4094
                                                                CIP
                                                                AC

PRINTED IN THE USA

TABLE OF CONTENTS

1

ORIGINS OF

KARATE

Hundreds of years ago, the people of Okinawa were peaceful farmers and fishermen. Often, bandits and Japanese armies would attack their small island. The Okinawans needed to defend themselves. They invented the martial art *te,* meaning "hands." Te used the hands and feet as weapons.

In the early 1600s, Japan took over Okinawa. The Japanese prohibited any Okinawan to possess weapons. The Okinawans had only their hands and feet to defend against attackers. Often, the attackers were samurai warriors who carried swords and wore thick wooden armor. The Japanese rulers also outlawed the practice of te, but the Okinawans continued to practice te in secret, gathering late at night, often in dark places like graveyards.

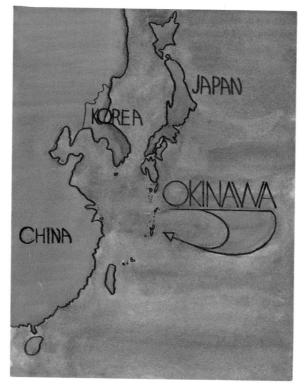

The martial art te, the predecessor of karate, *originated on the island of Okinawa.*

Some Okinawans were so skilled at te that they could defeat sword-bearing samurai warriors.

Okinawan martial arts were taught by people who had risen to the rank of master. The master would teach only a few students at a time. This made it easier to practice in secret. The master would teach only those students who he knew could keep a secret.

Okinawans continued to practice te, but until the early 1900s, few people outside of Okinawa knew of the art.

2

In the late 1800s, Kanryo Higashionna was a sailor on an Okinawan ship. Higashionna's ship, the *Shinko-Sen*, was a ship that traded with China. On one of the visits to China, Higashionna saw a child fall into the water. Higashionna dived into the water and saved the boy from drowning.

After saving the child, Higashionna walked with the boy to his house. The boy's father was a famous *kung fu* master, named Liu. Liu was so happy that his son was saved that he offered Higashionna a reward. Higashionna asked to become Liu's student.

Higashionna stayed in China and studied kung fu with Liu for 15 years. At the end of that time, Higashionna returned to his home in Okinawa. He became a teacher of martial arts. Higashionna combined Okinawan te with the kung fu he had learned in China.

In the early 1900s, Okinawan masters publicly demonstrated te in Japan. Soon after, the name "te" was changed to "karate," meaning "empty hands." In the 1930s, other names were added to distinguish the different styles of karate that developed as karate spread through Okinawa and Japan.

Kanryo Higashionna, an Okinawan sailor, once saved a Chinese child from drowning. The child's father rewarded Higashionna by teaching him kung fu. Higashionna returned to Okinawa and combined kung fu with Okinawan te.

3

THE FATHER OF MODERN OKINAWAN KARATE: CHOJUN MIYAGI

Master Higashionna's best student was Chojun Miyagi. Miyagi was a wealthy young man who was able to dedicate his entire life to the study of martial arts. Before Miyagi died in 1953, he taught many Okinawans. Master Miyagi became known as the father of modern karate.

Like his teacher, Master Miyagi did much to improve the art of karate. Miyagi traveled to China to study with kung fu masters. The more Miyagi learned of kung fu, the more he blended it with karate. After studying martial arts in China for many years, Miyagi returned to Okinawa and taught karate until he died.

In 1930, Master Miyagi sent one of his best students, Jinan Shinzato, to represent their school at the first martial arts convention. The convention was held in Kyoto, Japan. When Shinzato arrived at the convention, he noticed that all of the other schools had long and impressive sounding names. Shinzato decided to tell Master Miyagi of the other names.

After hearing of the names of other martial arts, Master Miyagi and his students decided to rename their art. They chose the name "Goju-Ryu Karate-Do." The new name meant "hard-soft karate way."

Chojun Miyagi dedicated his entire life to the study of martial arts. He is considered to be the father of modern Okinawan karate.

4

THE
M
E
A
N
I
N
G

OF THE NAME: GOJU-RYU KARATE-DO

There were many reasons for choosing the name "Goju-Ryu," meaning "hard-soft." One reason for the "hard-soft" part of the name was because Goju-Ryu karate combined the *soft* kung fu blocks and the *hard* strikes of Okinawan te. Another reason was the practice of striking a hard target with a soft weapon, and striking a soft target with a hard weapon.

When striking a hard target, karate students use soft weapons. Here, a student uses his palm against the jaw of an opponent.

Skilled karate students strike soft targets with hard weapons. Here, a student executes a closed-fist punch to the abdomen of an opponent.

Hard targets are those parts of the body that are solid, such as the head or face. Hard weapons are those parts of the body that are firm, such as the fists. Soft targets are less solid places like the stomach, or throat. Soft weapons are those parts of the body that are more flexible, like the palm of the hand or the knife-edge (outside) of the foot.

If a person skilled in Goju-Ryu karate were going to strike a hard target, like the face, he would use a soft weapon, such as the palm of his hand. If he were going to strike a soft target, like the stomach, he would use a hard weapon, such as his fist.

5

THE FATHER OF JAPANESE KARATE: GINCHIN

F U N A K O S H I

Another important figure in the history of karate was Ginchin Funakoshi. Funakoshi was born in Okinawa. When he was a boy in school, one of his best friends was the son of an Okinawan karate master. Funakoshi began to study karate when he was 13. Ten years later, Funakoshi was considered a karate expert.

Funakoshi was also a schoolteacher and a poet. He wrote many poems using the pen name Shoto, which meant "waving pine trees." Funakoshi continued to teach, write poetry and practice karate until 1917. In that year, the admiral of the Japanese navy was visiting Okinawa. Demonstrations of karate were scheduled for the admiral, and Funakoshi was invited to give one of the demonstrations.

The admiral was so impressed with Funakoshi's demonstration that he told the emperor of the amazing fighting skill he had seen while in Okinawa. The curious emperor invited Funakoshi to give a demonstration at his castle in Kyoto. Everyone who saw Funakoshi's demonstrations was fascinated with the Okinawan art of karate.

Eventually Funakoshi established the first school of karate in Japan. Funakoshi named his school Shoto-Kan, meaning "the school of Shoto." Shotokan karate became the world's most popular style of Japanese karate.

Ginchin Funakoshi opened the first Japanese school of karate. Funakoshi was also a schoolteacher and a poet.

6

THE SPREAD

Even after karate achieved popularity in Japan, it was a long time before there was much interest in Okinawan or Japanese martial arts in the Western world. A few people knew of the Japanese art of *judo,* but very few people had heard of karate. It was not until the end of World War II that many Americans were exposed to karate.

When the American military occupied Japan after World War II, General Douglas MacArthur ordered a ban on the practice of all martial arts. By 1951, the ban was lifted and Americans began to see demonstrations of karate. The American military was impressed with karate. They began to teach karate techniques as part of hand-to-hand combat training.

OF KARATE FROM ASIA

Many American soldiers were exposed to karate while stationed in Japan and Okinawa after World War II. Some American soldiers studied karate and then returned to the U.S. and taught others.

Many of the students who practice karate today are taught by American servicemen, who learned karate while stationed in Okinawa or Japan.

In the early 1950s, Ginchin Funakoshi, the man who introduced karate to Japan, gave many demonstrations at American military bases. At the same time, American troops in Okinawa were exposed to Okinawan karate. Some of the American soldiers who learned karate in Okinawa and Japan taught karate when they returned to the United States.

7

T
H
E

D
O
J
O

A school of karate is called a *dojo*. The karate teacher is called *sensei*. A student of karate is called a *karateka*. Both students and teachers wear a white uniform called a *gi*.

Today, students of karate have belts to distinguish their rank and level of proficiency. Long ago there was no established system of rank. Later, two colors of belts, white and black, were used. White was the color of the beginner. More advanced students wore black belts. Eventually more colored belts were introduced to reward students for achievement and to further distinguish levels of rank.

In addition to belts, age also determines rank among students of the same belt color. Senior students are called *senpai*. All other students are called *kohai*.

A sensei (center) and two karatekas bow before training begins.

Under the watchful eyes of the sensei, the karatekas train. Here, a brown belt has blocked an attack from a senior student.

Students of karate must always be courteous and respectful both inside and outside the dojo. The students' behavior, both good and bad, is a reflection on their dojo. Displays of ill temper are never tolerated. No student may use knowledge of karate to bully others – doing so might get the student expelled from the dojo.

8

T
H
E
K
A
T
A

All of the movements of karate – punching, blocking, kicking and the various stances – can be found in the *kata*. A kata is a series of movements, in which the student defends himself against one or more imaginary opponents. To someone unfamiliar with martial arts, the performance of a kata looks like a sort of dance.

There is much more to a kata than simply memorizing the moves in their proper order. In some of the longer katas, just learning all of the movements is hard enough. In addition to performing the movements in the proper order, a student of karate must execute each move perfectly.

In traditional Okinawan karate, a student might learn only one new kata per year. Often it takes the entire year for the student to learn the kata, and it can take many years to fully master even the simplest kata. When the karate teacher thinks the student has learned a kata, he might teach him a new one. The student might also move up in rank.

All of the movements of karate are found in the kata.

Here, a brown belt performs kata, while two black belts observe.

9

**BEGINNING
TRAINING:**

S
T
A
N
C
E
S

One of the first things a student of karate must learn is how to stand properly. There are many different stances in karate, and posture is important. Strong posture insures that each technique can be performed better and with more power.

Many stances are named after animals, such as the horse stance and the cat stance. Most stances are difficult at first. To a beginner, some stances can be very uncomfortable and hard to maintain for more than a minute or two. When a student improves his ability to stand properly, he also improves his balance and strength.

From the basic stance, many techniques can be launched. Here, a chest-level punch is thrown with the left arm, while the right arm is poised and ready to deliver a second punch.

This stance, sometimes called the horse stance, improves leg strength, balance and posture. An advanced student of karate can maintain this stance for long periods of time.

The basic karate stance begins with the feet approximately shoulder-width apart and turned slightly inward. To someone unfamiliar with karate, the basic stance appears odd or clumsy. Some people have described the stance as "pigeon-toed." After the student has gotten used to the basic stance, it provides improved balance, making it harder for an opponent to knock the student over.

Each stance has a different purpose, depending on whether a block, punch or kick is intended. Some stances apply to both blocking and striking.

10

DEFENSE:

B
L
O
C
K
S

Blocking an opponent's attack is every bit as important as being able to deliver an attack. This is why every student of karate spends a lot of time learning how to block. There are blocks for virtually every kind of attack. There are even blocks to defend against an attacker with a weapon.

There are three basic blocks that a beginning student learns. One block defends against an attack to the head. Another defends the chest, and the third defends lower parts of the body. These blocks are simple, but a student must practice them over and over to be able to execute them fast enough to stop a punch or a kick.

The man on the right has blocked a punch to his head. This is one of the first blocks that a student of karate learns.

The man on the left has blocked a chest-level punch. All blocks require speed and timing.

Using one of the simple blocks to defend against a strike to the head, a student will throw his forearm up to a point just above the forehead. The forearm will be parallel to the floor, with the elbow pointing toward the ceiling. At the same time the block is executed, the other arm is drawn up under the armpit, so that if a second block is needed, the arm is poised and ready to go.

Once a student becomes more experienced in karate, he will be able to block and strike back at the same time. Some block and strike combinations are so effective that they can stop an attacker almost instantly.

11

SPEARS AND HAMMERS: HAND

TECHNIQUES

The way a person skilled in karate uses his hands and arms is very different from the way the arms are used in Western fighting styles, such as boxing. In Western-style boxing, a fist is made and the entire front, or knuckle portion, of the fist is used. In karate, there are many different punches and strikes.

The most common punch begins with the fist tucked firmly under the armpit, with the palm side facing up. The forearm is parallel to the ground. Once the punch is launched, the arm is thrust forward, and, immediately before impact, the fist is turned so that the palm side is facing downward. Only the first two knuckles make impact with the target. This reduces the surface area of the impact and focuses the power of the punch.

An advanced student of karate demonstrates a complex hand technique.

The karate punch originated at a time when Okinawan fighters had to use their bare hands to punch through the wooden armor of a samurai warrior.

In karate, there are many other hand techniques used for striking an opponent. Some of them include using a closed fist, but some strikes are made with open hands. All of them are designed to transform the hands into weapons. That is why they have names like the spear-hand, or hammer-fist. The spear-hand was developed at a time when Okinawans had to use their hands to pierce the wooden armor of Japanese samurai warriors.

12

THE SNAP, KNIFE-EDGE AND JUMPING

SIDE-KICK

Like many other Eastern martial arts, karate has become well-known for use of the legs and feet in fighting. Unlike *tae kwon do*, and some styles of kung fu, traditional Okinawan karate uses few high-level kicks. Most kicks are aimed at waist level or below.

At the same time he is launching a kick to his opponent's abdomen, the man on the right is prepared to follow up with a punch.

In the 1600s, Okinawan fighters used the jumping side-kick to knock samurai warriors off of their horses.

There is a great variety of kicks in karate. As with hand techniques, kicks were originally designed to transform body parts – the legs and feet – into weapons. During the early Japanese invasions of Okinawa, there were stories of karate experts who could knock a rider off of a horse by executing a jumping side-kick. Even today, the outside of the foot is still referred to as the "knife-edge."

The most basic kick is the snap kick. The snap kick is not a straight-leg kick, like that used by a punter kicking a football. The snap kick begins with the raising of the foot, until the portion of the leg between the hip and the knee is parallel to the ground. The foot is tucked under the hip, and the toes are curled up toward the shin. From there, the foot is thrust forward. Impact occurs with the ball of the foot.

13

THE MENTAL EXERCISES: BREATHING AND MEDITATION

There is more to karate than just stances, blocking, punching and kicking. First the student must have the right attitude toward karate. A student must respect the art of karate and never use it for bad purposes. Once the proper attitude and respect are achieved, there are other mental aspects of karate.

Meditation is a type of deep concentration. Deep breathing is important in meditation. Karate classes begin with *mukuso*, a brief period of meditation. The purpose of mukuso is to empty the mind of any thoughts not related to karate. All of the techniques in karate require concentration, and some are even dangerous. To train properly, a student should be thinking only about the technique he is performing at the moment.

The *kiai* is another mental aspect of karate. The kiai is a loud yell that is shouted at the same moment a block or strike is executed. The breath used to shout the kiai should come from deep within the abdomen. The purpose of the kiai is to focus all of one's physical and mental energy into the block or strike. A kiai is also useful because sometimes it can frighten attackers and make them lose their concentration – and maybe even run away.

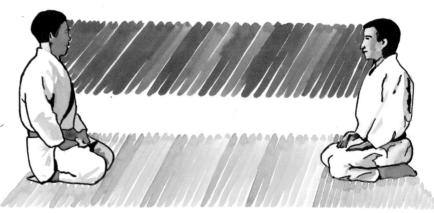

All karate classes begin with mukuso, a brief period of meditation.

The kiai, a loud yell shouted along with a punch, kick or block, helps to focus both physical and mental energy.

14

KARATE

TODAY

Today, karate is popular throughout the world. There are thousands of schools of karate in the United States. Almost every U.S. community has at least one dojo. Both Japanese and traditional Okinawan styles are practiced.

Although karate was originally practiced by men, today it is equally popular with women. Many people enjoy training in karate for a variety of reasons including self-defense, as well as keeping physically fit.

Many schools of karate are members of large associations that organize tournaments where students can compete against one another. Some of these organizations have members in many different countries and are recognized by experts in Japan and Okinawa.

Worldwide interest in karate is expected to grow in the future.

Karate is useful as a means of self-defense, as well as a means of keeping physically fit.

Today, thousands of people throughout the world practice karate.

dojo: a school where karate is taught.

gi: a white uniform worn by students and teachers of karate.

Goju-Ryu Karate-Do: "hard-soft karate way"; Okinawan karate became known as "hard-soft" because it used both hard techniques of Okinawan te and soft techniques of Chinese kung fu.

karateka: a student of karate.

kata: a series of movements in which a person practicing karate defends himself against one or more imaginary attackers.

kiai: a loud yell that accompanies the execution of a karate technique, and serves the purpose of focusing energy and frightening an opponent.

kohai: a beginning student of karate.

martial arts: any form of military training; often the term refers to empty-handed fighting, as well as to the various forms of exercises and sports developed from ancient fighting skills.

mukuso: a short period of meditation at the beginning and end of a class in karate.

senpai: an advanced student of karate.

sensei: a teacher of karate.

Shoto-Kan: "The School of Shoto"; this was the first school of karate in Japan.

te: "hands"; a martial art developed in Okinawa that uses the hands and feet as weapons.

G
L
O
S
S
A
R
Y